Wanted, Dead or Alive

A grown-up's fairy tales for the ever young at heart

Rene Mugnier

NEWMAN SPRINGS PUBLISHING
320 Broad Street
Red Bank, NJ 07701

First originally published by Newman Springs Publishing 2024

ISBN 979-8-89308-344-6 (Paperback)
ISBN 979-8-89308-346-0 (Hardcover)
ISBN 979-8-89308-345-3 (Digital)

Printed in the United States of America

Wanted, dead or alive

René Mugnier

May 2022

Anecdote

Buckaroo Bob, the horseback bounty hunter, was hauling the outlaw Snoring Snake Bocage, dead for days, through scorching sands. The desert was so dry that even vultures thought twice about flying over. Buckaroo couldn't resist cracking jokes to keep spirits up.

"Looks like old Bocage finally found a way to nap without causing trouble," he teased Snoring Snake, who remained silent.

As they crossed the desert, Buckaroo and Whiskey, the hunter's horse, encountered a group of perplexed cacti seemingly whispering among themselves in amazement.

Buckaroo chuckled. "Even the cacti are commenting on Slim's ultimate adventure."

Eventually, Whiskey turned to the other and said, "You know, I hope we're getting paid as much as we're traveling. It's been a while since I've seen a decent pasture!"

Wanted, dead or alive

Reward: 1,000 shekels

Noah

Misdeeds
Based on hypotheses not at all scientific, he created an unimaginable ecological disaster by destroying entire forests to create an ark never built before

What would you have done in my place? We don't joke when He asks you to do something.

Anecdote

And God said, "Noah, build me an ark and save the world and the animals." But as it turned out, it was more like "Go chop down every tree you've ever seen!"—a recycling project gone wrong.

Amid those divine directives, Noah ordered two of every animal on Amazon, causing chaos as a flood of dirty cardboard engulfed his ark. An additional environmental disaster?

Mother Nature heard about the ark idea and said, "Hold my ecosystem!" Now we have a forestless wonder, the world's first ark-nature disaster! This is most likely not the first time that God and Mother Nature clashed.

Wanted, dead or alive

Reward: 10,000 florins

Michelangelo

Misdeeds
- Draws and paints sexually explicit graffiti on the ceilings and walls of churches
- Installs large sculptures on public roads that obstruct traffic, armed with chisel and hammer

Description
- Solitary, bearded, and mustached Italian male
- Difficult and pretentious personality (he believes he's already what people will say about him later)
- Dabbles in architecture
- Dissects cadavers, etc.

Anecdote

Once upon a time, in a small Italian village, there was a peculiar man known as the phantom artist. This man, with a full beard and a trademark mustache, was a lone wolf with an attitude as grand as the cathedrals he dreamed of building.

His name was whispered in every corner, but no one had ever caught a glimpse of his face. The villagers would wake up each morning and discover curious graffiti on their walls and ceilings—images so vivid and wild that they sparked as much conversation as controversy.

It was even said that he had been caught in the morgue dissecting corpses to study their organs, without sewing back the bodies. Not only did he leave his artistic mark on the church ceilings, but the phantom artist also had a habit of leaving enormous sculptures in the middle of the cobbled streets, causing real traffic jams!

His identity remained a mystery, but his notoriety grew so large that the mayor put up a Wanted notice, offering a hefty purse of ten thousand florins for his capture, dead or alive. The poster described him as a solitary Italian male who was difficult and pretentious, with the conviction that one day, everyone would call him a genius well ahead of his time.

Rumors said he wielded a hammer and chisel with the finesse of a maestro, and he was as elusive as the Nayaise mist. As the search for the phantom artist continued, the villagers couldn't help but marvel at each new work of art, secretly hoping he would never be caught.

Each day promised the excitement of a new creation, turning their sleepy village into a canvas of mystery and art. The phantom artist had become the legend they all cherished, the unseen maestro who transformed the ordinary into the extraordinary. We now know that this man was Michelangelo, now famous for reasons other than those during his time.

Wanted, dead or alive

10,000 riyals

Aïcha

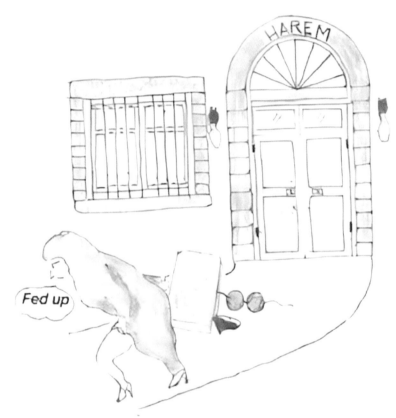

Description
She was wearing
a blue niqab when she
disappeared.

Misdeeds (incomplete)
- Bolted from the harem without leaving an address
- Drove a car without a chaperone
- Talks back to her master without permission
- Zero chuckles when her master makes silly faces
- Laughs when he says serious things
- Attempts to swing back when hit, etc....

Anecdote

This is the story of Aïcha's escape.

In a far-off spot, there was Aïcha, this vibrant Saudi gal, cooped up in a harem. She wasn't feeling that vibe, dreaming instead of roaming the streets of Nay, where she'd met some cool dudes at La Grange. She craved a taste of real life. The harem, run by a tough guy named Abdul Ben Tatave, was like a gilded cage.

One night, Aïcha got this crazy idea. She started spreading rumors about some hidden treasure in the harem, knowing it'd light up Abdul.

She told everyone, "There's this ancient treasure right under our noses!" The whole place got stirred up, and Abdul totally fell for it.

That night, Aïcha convinced Abdul to let everyone tear the place apart looking for the "treasure."

While they were creating a massive ruckus, Aïcha sneaked into Abdul's office, nabbed the keys, and quietly unlocked the main door.

As the sun came up, with everyone still busy hunting for the nonexistent treasure, Aïcha made her escape, blending into the early-morning crowd. She was finally free, living the life she had been longing for.

Back at the harem, when they realized Aïcha had split, they were all floored. The story of Aïcha's slick escape spread like wildfire—a tale of brains trumping brawn.

And Abdul Ben Tatave? He learned a tough lesson: never underestimate a woman with a plan and a hunger for the real world.

Lucky for him, he consoled himself with the other women of the harem.

Wanted, dead or alive

10,000 shekels

Moses

Misdeeds

When Moses parted the waters of the Red Sea, he also caused a traffic jam for marine life. He is accused of being the cause of the extinction of numerous marine species.

Extraordinary ecological disaster. Forget global warming; Moses brought you climatic chaos of unprecedented intensity.

René Magrie

Anecdote

God's middle manager, Moses, is a divine influencer claiming he has a direct line to heaven and holds the tablets with the commandments (the ancestors of the iPads) as the directives to follow, like a never-ending stream of the boss's emails, constantly receiving updates from the heavens. Burning bushes are the latest trend—a voice-activated gadget that everyone wants, complete with a hologram feature. Obviously, there is the need for a "heavenly help desk" for commandment confusion.

Does "Thou shalt not steal" apply to stealing a pen from the office?

Who needs a democratic process when you have a direct line to the big boss? He bypassed the whole "Let's have a vote" process and went straight to divine dictation.

One last thought for those who have trouble packing for a two-week vacation: imagine packing for a wandering of forty years.

Wanted, dead or alive

Reward: 20,000 florins

Galileo

My God, I know that I have little problems with the church, but please arrange for them to arrive at the same time.

Misdeeds
- Pretends that the Earth orbits around the sun.
- Throws objects from the top of the Leaning Tower of Pisa without permission or protection for the sidewalks.
- Insists that mathematics is more useful than Latin.
- In church, he looks at the ceiling instead of listening to the priest's sermon.

Anecdote

Galileo was the ultimate party pooper of his time. He had this wild idea that the Earth isn't the center of the universe, and he just couldn't resist crashing the geocentric party that had been going on for centuries. Picture him strolling into a medieval disco, where everyone's dancing around the Earth; and as he waltzes in, he shouts, "Hey, folks, guess what? Earth isn't the cosmic superstar you think it is!"

He goes on to ruin everyone's fun, trying to convince them that the Earth actually revolves around the Sun. Imagine him as the guy who brings a telescope to a medieval jousting tournament and starts pointing it at the stars while everyone else is jousting.

Galileo, the original buzzkill of the Renaissance!

Galileo, the dude who was ace at stirring up trouble back in his days.

He was the ultimate party pooper of his time.

He dropped this wild idea that Earth isn't the universe's belly button, and he just couldn't help but crash the geocentric party that had been raging for ages.

Picture this guy crashing a medieval nightclub where everyone's grooving to Earth as the center; and *boom*, he swaggers in, shouting, "Yo, mates, guess what? Earth ain't the star of the show!"

Imagine again this guy bringing back a telescope in that society of which a small part, religious and educated, believes that the Sun revolves around the Earth, and the rest of the world still believes that the Earth is flat.

No wonder the church was fed up.

Wanted, dead or alive

Reward: 5000 pesetas

Pablo Picasso

Description

A dude mad, talented, using models with disabilities and blowing up their flaws big time. Switches up his style like nobody's business [all over the place with his thoughts]! Gives zero flips about what anyone else thinks.

Anecdote

In the heart of Paris, Picasso was all set to paint a new face. This chic lady walked into his studio, looking all classy and ready to be slapped onto canvas.

She stripped and chills on this fancy sofa, light hittin' her just right. Picasso's scopin' her out, eyeing every little detail. The room's vibing with the smell of paints and buzzing with some mad creative energy.

Picasso gets crackin', his brush going wild on the canvas. He's chuckin' in bold lines and popping colors, capturing this lady's vibe. It ain't just a painting; it's a whole mood—a slice of life getting zapped onto that canvas.

Hours flew by, and the world outside was just a blur. Picasso was in the zone, his masterpiece coming to life under his genius hands. When he whacked on that final stroke, he stepped back, all dizzy with his work.

The lady got up, totally blown away. She wasn't just looking at herself in that painting; she was seeing her soul, all thanks to Picasso's magic. Right there in that Parisian studio, a simple moment became legendary, all immortalized by the master himself.

Wanted, dead or alive

Reward: 10,000.00 francs

Louis Pasteur

Description
    He is an excellent chemist who has made his reputation on wine and beer.

Misdeeds
    He was found practicing voodoo medicine on a large scale without having filled out the application forms in three hundred copies nor the forty-eight months of waiting required by the Ministry of Health after all the mandatory tests were found positive.

Anecdote

Louis Pasteur was brewing up some crazy stuff in his lab way before the whole vaccine craze hit. Dude was in there, mixing and shaking like a chef on a cooking show, trying to figure out a fix to keep folks from dropping dead.

He's got this bonkers idea, right? He took some nasty juice from a sick cow, and he was like, "If I mess with this just right, maybe it'll stop the crew from catching the same bug."

He gave it a whirl, then hit up a brave—or maybe not-so-smart—guy with it. (Could be he messed up a bunch before, but ain't nobody braggin' about that.) Everyone was freaking out, waiting to see if this dude was gonna bite the dust or turn into a hero. *Bam!* The guy was strolling around, healthier than ever, not a sick day in sight.

Pasteur was walking tall; his vaccine was the hottest thing since sliced bread. But the downers were whispering, "Man, that brew's just witchcraft." (Later on, their descendants will react similarly to the vaccine against COVID-19.) But Pasteur? He couldn't care less. He was like, "Call it what you want, but I just silenced sickness."

That's how Pasteur, with a gentle shot in the ass, served up a "Don't get sick" like a maestro.

Wanted, dead or alive

Reward: 1,000 ducats

Saint George

Misdeeds
    He invents stories to justify the extermination of endangered species, and at the same time, he takes advantage of the gory story to get canonized.

Anecdote

In a realm shadowed by forgotten magic and whispered legends, there existed a knight, Sir George, draped in crimson and gold, his name upon every bard's tongue, a hero to the people, a saint in the making. Yet beneath the laurels of victory lay a secret gnawed by guilt and regret. The dragon he had slain, a magnificent beast with scales that shimmered like emeralds in the sunlight, was not merely a creature of fire and fury but the last of its kind—a guardian of the earth, whose breath gave life to the forests and whose heartbeats echoed the rhythms of the world. The beast had been misunderstood, a symbol of the world's delicate balance.

Sir George, driven by the promise of immortality in the annals of history and the church's golden offer of sainthood, faced the dragon in what the songs called the battle of the ages. With a lance forged from star metal and a shield as unyielding as his resolve, George confronted the creature.

The duel was fierce; flames painted the skies, and the earth trembled. In the end, it was the dragon who faltered, succumbing to mortal wounds, its blood seeping into the soil it had sworn to protect.

Sir George returned a hero, yet the gleam of his armor seemed less bright, the cheers of the crowd hollow to his ears. As he walked the cobblestone streets, a whisper followed him—a whisper that grew into a roar.

The knight, now Saint George, realized the dragon had been the last guardian of a dying magic, a protector of a world he had sworn to serve. His fame, built upon the bones of the last dragon, became his burden. He had extinguished a flame that could not be rekindled. This was not a tale of triumph but a stark reminder of the price of glory.

In the quiet of his chamber, Saint George would often sit, a figure etched with sorrow, wondering if the dragon's final roar was one of defiance or a plea for understanding. He had slain a dragon to become a legend, but at what cost?

Wanted, dead or alive

Reward: 1,000 pfennigs

Johannes Gutenberg

Misdeeds
- His invention engenders revolutions and allows the spreading of false information, biased and obscene, on a large scale.
- Floods public spaces and oceans with detritus.
- Fills mailboxes with junk mail and useless items made with the trees of our forests.

Anecdote

In the lush valleys of Mainz, in a time when the written word was as precious as the jewels in a crown, Johannes Gutenberg embarked on an endeavor that would forever alter the course of history. With the cogs and wheels of his invention—the printing press—he unleashed the power of mass communication. Yet as the first pages began to spill out in great numbers, Gutenberg was unaware that he was planting the seeds of a far-reaching and darker side of human expression. His invention, which first brought enlightenment and knowledge to the masses, gradually also became the vessel for less savory outputs.

As decades turned into centuries, the proliferation of printed material gave rise to a new form of detritus. The streets of cities became flooded not just with the enlightening words of philosophers but also with the lurid whispers of scandal sheets and the unwanted clutter of advertisements. Forests, sentinels of the natural world, began to fall at an alarming rate, their demise fueling the ever-growing demand for paper.

In the shadows of the alleys, what was once the noble pursuit of literature began to morph into unsavory pornographic images and texts. The same presses that once printed the Bible now churned out material that made the pious blush. The world was awash with a deluge of paper, some bearing knowledge and art and much of it carrying the weight of humanity's baser instincts, filling our mailboxes.

Gutenberg's revolution spread into every corner of human life, for both good and ill.

Gutenberg had probably imagined spreading knowledge, not horoscopes and Sunday's jokes.

Thus, Gutenberg's revolution, supposed to enlighten the world, also cluttered it a little.

For each philosophy book, there were ten thousand flyers for shoe sales.

That's Gutenberg's legacy. As with every invention, we always find an intelligent user who goes to the library to read what interests him and uses the flyers to start his fire.

Wanted, dead or alive

Reward: 1,000 maravedis

Christophe Colomb

Misdeeds
- Persecuted, enslaved, and robbed indigenous peoples
- Imposed his religion and transmitted all sorts of European diseases

For his defense, he claimed the following.

After sixty-one days of an extreme difficult journey at sea with ninety men, I discovered an unknown continent that will later harbor the poor, the courageous, and the unwanted of the old world. One day, mediocre individuals leading pitiful lives will find good reasons to condemn me.

Description
- Italian adventurer of violent nature

René
Mageiss

Anecdote

Once upon a time, there was an Italian adventurer named Christophe Colomb, though he preferred to be called Chris, feeling it gave him a bit of modern flair. Chris was a man of particularly dramatic flair, always seen with a feathered cap and a cape that fluttered as if in a constant sea breeze.

He had a reputation; some might say he was notorious for a certain recklessness when it came to treasure maps and compasses.

Chris, with his trusty crew of ninety, who were more seasick than seaworthy, set sail on a journey that would make even the hardiest of sailors shake in his breeches.

They braved storms that could turn a man's beard white, waves as tall as the Pyrenees mountains, and a diet of biscuits so hard they could be mistaken for the ship's decking.

After sixty-one days, with their sea legs well and truly worn in, they stumbled upon a new continent, which Chris promptly claimed.

The new land was a sight for sore eyes (and other parts afflicted by European ailments). Chris envisioned it as a haven for the poor, the bold, and the outcasts of the old world—essentially, a paradise for those who had been given the boot or had escaped it (as well as those like him, who wanted to fill their pockets).

As time went on and his exploits became the stuff of poorly researched history books, Chris found himself at the center of some rather unflattering critiques. The once-celebrated adventurer was now criticized by armchair historians who had never even left their own backyards.

In his defense, Chris, with the dramatic flair of a seasoned actor in a spotlight, proclaimed, "Ladies and gentlemen, yes, I might have had a tiny, little, almost insignificant role in the misfortunes of the indigenous peoples. And all right, maybe I was a bit too enthusiastic about sharing our European…'hospitality.' But let's not forget the good stuff! I gave you a place where the daring can wear socks in his sandals, and the outcasts can find solace in all-you-can-eat buffets!"

Wanted, dead or alive

Reward: 1,000 gold pieces

Genghis Khan

Misdeeds

He is the brutal and bloodthirsty emperor responsible for the death through destruction, extermination, or famine of more than 40 million people.

I go to the temple two times a day. I haven't slit anyone's throat or raped anyone for more than ten years. Why are they still after me?

Genghis Khan is puzzled as to why he is still being pursued for his historical actions, given his current "peaceful" habits.

Anecdote

In a world not quite like our own, Genghis Khan had somehow managed to slip through the cracks of time and ended up in the twenty-first century. After realizing that pillaging and conquering were no longer the norms, he decided to turn over a new leaf and live a life of peace.

He took up meditation, joined a local knitting club, and even volunteered at the community garden every weekend.

Genghis, now going by the name Gary, couldn't understand why the local historical society kept giving him dirty looks.

He thought perhaps they were just passionate about history, or maybe they didn't like his new organic composting methods. He decided to ask them directly during the society's annual "Medieval Times" fair.

As he approached, wearing his hand-knitted vest and holding a big dish of couscous as a peace offering, the oldest lady pointed at him, whispering, "That's him, the ruthless conqueror!"

Gary was confused. "Ruthless? I even use eco-friendly yarn for my knitting," he protested.

The head of the society, a stern woman with an impressive knowledge of the thirteenth century, confronted him. "You may have fooled others with your so-called peaceful habits, but we know who you really are, Genghis Khan!"

Gary chuckled, adjusting his reading glasses. "Madam, I assure you, the only thing I'm interested in conquering these days is the battle against weeds in my vegetable garden in Dartmouth."

In an attempt to clear his name, Gary invited the entire historical society to a "get to know the real Genghis" barbecue. There, they saw him tenderly caring for his bonsai trees and joyfully losing at croquet. By the end of the day, the society members were charmed.

They still kept a close eye on him, just in case he reverted to his old ways.

Wanted, dead or alive

Reward: $10,000

John Wayne

Misdeeds
    He has killed several people without trial and without a jury in his films, lawless poor people who didn't merit more than a few days in jail.

I had warned you well. I said, "Don't touch my steak." The West was not easy.

Anecdote

In the sun-scorched town of Fox Run on the Slocum, notorious for its outlaws, John "Iron Sights" Wayne was a retired actor who'd taken to ranch life with a fervor that matched his former stage intensity. His steak at the local saloon was sacred, and he'd often barked, "Let no man dare lay a finger on my steak!"

One unlucky drifter, mistaking the steak for communal fare, reached out, and chaos erupted. Iron Sights, with the speed of a striking rattlesnake, drew his fork and pinned the man's hand to the table.

"That's your one and only warning," he thundered.

The tale spread like wildfire, and by nightfall, a Wanted poster pegged him as a savage with a $10,000 bounty. Bounty hunters, drawn by the promise of gold, soon found that Iron Sights was no actor-turned-gentle-farmer but a legend who'd defend his claim with a brutal finality that left many a man wary of ever touching another's meal in Fox Run on the Slocum again.

Wanted, dead or alive

Reward: 1,000 hryvnias

The Angel La Chkoumoune

Description
La Chkoumoune is totally unpredictable. He leads us into unpleasant situations that often defy logic and are undeserved—no one excluded. His great enemy, the angel Baraka, succeeded in all his tasks.

Anecdote

In the township of Nay La Gracieuse, woven into the fabric of biblical legend, dwelled an angel named La Chkoumoune. Her presence was a peculiar whirlwind that transformed ordinary life into a cavalcade of unintended farce. This celestial being, devoid of malice or mischief, unwittingly tipped the scales of daily life toward chaotic misadventures. The townspeople, in a blend of exasperation and affection, issued a Wanted poster offering a bounty of 1,000 hryvnias for the capture of this heavenly buffoon not out of spite but out of a craving for the sweet simplicity of their yesteryears.

Contrasting La Chkoumoune's capricious influence was the angel Baraka, whose divine activities were marked by flawless execution. Baraka watched with a mix of disapproval and amusement his counterpart, whose heart was pure but whose hands, alas, were not.

Yet as the astonishment settled, the citizens of Nay La Gracieuse discovered an unexpected allure in the unpredictability of La Chkoumoune. They grew weary of the boring perfection rendered by Baraka's holy touch. The monotony of ceaseless success and pious predictability gave way to a longing for the spice of fallibility.

In a collective change of heart, the people dismantled the Wanted notices, expressing forgiveness over La Chkoumoune's blunders. They cherished her spirit and unintended comedy but with gentle wisdom, they steered her away from tasks of consequence, lovingly relegating her to the role of town mascot—a reminder that even in divinity, there is room for imperfection. (They're still watching her extra carefully for any dangerous missteps.)

Wanted, dead or alive

1,000 drachmas

Archangel Gabriella

Description
She has a very particular sign: she's very blonde. She often visits Los Angeles.

Misdeeds
- She announced to Mary that she would have a daughter.
- Contrary to Gabriel, Gabriella gives false information; she is responsible for the delay of the wise men to whom she had given a wrong address.

Anecdote

Once upon a time, in the sky above Bethlehem, there was a bit of an uproar. Archangel Gabriella, known for her stunningly blonde hair and her tendency to get her prophecies a tad mixed up, had caused quite a celestial stir. Gabriella, who fancied herself as the self-proclaimed celestial courier, had zipped off to the wise men with a message of utmost importance. But in the flurry of her wings, she sent the poor sages on a sled ride to Alaska.

The wise men, not amused by the icy detour, were now three months behind schedule. They arrived just in time for the circumcision instead of the Nativity; and instead of frankincense, they brought a small razor, some diesel fuel, and remedies for frostbite.

In a separate incident, she had cheerfully announced to Mary that she would be expecting a little girl. The heavens had prepared pink clouds. When little Jesus arrived, the choirs had to quickly switch their songs, and the pink clouds were repurposed for a sunset.

The divine council had, had enough and issued a Wanted poster with a reward of 1,000 drachmas for her celestial capture and to get her out of the picture. There's a rumor that she's planning a new prophecy involving a certain groundhog and an extended winter...if she can just get the date right this time.

Wanted, dead or alive

Reward: 1,000 euros or 3 billion cookies

Santa Claus

Misdeeds
- Spoils the children of the rich
- Neglects the children of the poor
- Bothers the firefighters to get him out of the chimneys when he gets stuck
- Compete illegally with Amazon
- Refuses to deliver to Ukraine or in Gaza

Anecdote

In the small, snow-dusted town of Belmont Sur Neige, there was an uproar that was about to turn the calm Christmas preparations upside down. A Wanted poster had appeared overnight on the town hall's notice board, and it wasn't just any poster—it was a "Wanted, Dead or Alive" call to capture none other than Santa Claus himself! The reward was $1,000 or an absurdly vast number of cookies.

The accusations were serious: spoiling rich kids, neglecting the poor, clumsily tangling in trees, and a suspicious partnership with Amazon. Not to mention, Santa was apparently refusing to deliver to Ukraine or Gaza.

As townsfolk gathered around, pointing at the poster, the mayor, Monsieur Bazooka, scratched his head in bewilderment. "We must get to the bottom of this," he declared.

Meanwhile, in the big field off Concord Avenue, the reindeer were gossiping.

"Did you hear? They think the old man is losing his marbles!" snickered Rudolphe, the reindeer with a nose not so red as it used to be.

"I heard he dropped his wallet during a test flight," Dasher added, trying not to laugh as Santa still had a nasty left hand.

The mystery deepened when the town's only art enthusiast, Mademoiselle Martine, noticed the signature at the bottom of the poster: René Mugnier. "That cannot be from him. He is too serious to produce that sort of garbage!" she exclaimed. "This must be the work of a prankster with a taste for surrealism!"

As the story of the wanted Santa spread, children started to believe that Santa was indeed on the run, turning their innocent eyes skyward, hoping to catch a glimpse of the elusive gift giver. Some even set out cookies not as a treat but as a clever trap; the old man was known to have a weakness for sweets.

On Christmas Eve, a figure was spotted on the rooftops, a round belly with bushy white-grey hair outlined against the moonlit sky.

"We've got him!" shouted the children, but as the figure descended, it was not Santa but Mayor Bazooka in a Santa suit, laughing heartily.

"Ho, ho, ho!" With a twinkle in his eye, he revealed the truth. The poster was a playful creation by the town's artists to bring a little extra cheer and mystery to the holiday season. And as for the real Santa? He was never on the run, of course. While the town was busy with their manhunt, he delivered the presents as silently and efficiently as ever. And to top it off, every child found an extra gift under the tree—a tiny wallet with a note.

Found it! Thanks for the laughs.

Santa

Wanted, dead or alive

Reward: 10,000 rands

Tarzan

Misdeeds

- Does not wear clothes over his genitalia
- Produces very loud cries with no obvious reasons that wake up and frighten the jungle animals
- Engages in questionable relationships with monkeys, among other animals

Anecdote

In the dense jungles along the Slocum, the animals had grown tired of Tarzan's crazy behavior. He was a bit of a legend in the forest, swinging from vine to vine; but lately, his early-morning yodels had become a bit too disruptive. The usually serene jungle was abuzz with gossip, and the animals became fed up and were plotting.

"Enough is enough!" grumbled the wise old elephant named Tatave. "We need our beauty sleep!"

So they put up a poster, a bit cheeky and with a substantial reward of 10,000 rands—a fortune in the animal kingdom.

The poster was a hit, pinned to the bark of the Baobab trees; it even featured a descriptive sketch of Tarzan, his hair wilder than the thorny bushes and his trademark yell causing quite the ruckus. The giraffe, the tallest, was enlisted to hang the posters high.

The monkeys? Well, they felt a bit conflicted. Tarzan was their friend, but they also loved a good prank. They scribbled some additional reasons for his "Wanted status, like his "questionable relationships" with some of them.

They chuckled. "It's complicated," they'd say, blushing under their fur.

Tarzan, upon seeing the poster, scratched his head, amused and slightly honored. "A reward for me? I must be famous!" He decided it was time to turn the tables. He organized a grand meeting, inviting every creature, from the smallest ant to the grumpiest rhino, named Georges.

"I've heard your concerns," he announced from his vine podium. "How about I schedule my yodeling and make my relationship with Coco legitimate? And in return, we can have weekly jungle parties!"

The animals murmured and nodded. The idea of a party with scheduled peace and quiet was too good to pass up. Tatave, the wise old elephant, stamped the ground in agreement—it was settled.

From that day on, Tarzan's yodels became the most awaited event in the jungle, and the parties were legendary. As for the reward, it was never claimed. Instead, it became a collective fund for the wildest jungle fiestas you could ever imagine. And the poster? It remained, a funny reminder of the time when the jungle tried to tame its most unruly yet beloved wild man.

Wanted, dead or alive

Reward: 100 gold coins

Snow White

Misdeeds
- Has strange relationships with a band of small, bearded men
- Has run away from the castle and invented an incredible sorcery story

I'm fed up with the boring castle life, my 7 dwarves are much more fun. (Snow White)

Description
She has very pale skin and is fragile but not as innocent as she claims to be.

Anecdote

Once upon a time, in a remote place called La Grange, there lived a sassy young lady known as Snow White. Snow White was not your typical damsel in distress, nor was she inclined toward a classic royal ending. In fact, she had developed a taste for her unique lifestyle among seven virile, bearded men small in stature but well-endowed, each rich in personality and more eccentric than the last.

Snow White's pale complexion was not just a sign of classic beauty but also the result of a sheltered life rather than fieldwork. It was said that she was slyer than a fox and could charm a grumpy old toad. She even organized the forest's first music festival, which some slanderers called an orgy, with creatures from the entire kingdom that excited the dwarves to the max.

However, her newfound independence plunged the kingdom into turmoil. Prince Charming, accustomed to timid virgins, was disconcerted by her lack of interest. In an attempt to win her back, he published a Wanted poster offering a reward of one hundred gold coins.

Unimpressed by the prince, Snow White was too busy partying with the dwarves and had started a small leather-goods business. The poster spread throughout the kingdom, attracting many adventurers and aspiring heroes. Stories of her charm made her a legend, a rebellious princess who preferred laughter and friendship over a boring castle atop a mountain with small windows.

In the end, Prince Charming decided to join Snow White and her friends for dinner. There, he acquired a taste for partying, discovered the joys of a boisterous dwarven banquet, and decided that sometimes, the best company is the one that laughs the loudest.

As for Snow White, she decided it was time to settle down—not because she was tired of working but because she wanted to marry the prince on her terms. She continued to dance, sing, and live joyfully, leaving behind a legacy of defiance and the legend of a princess who made her own rules. They had a beautiful life together, filled with lots of sex and very few children. However, it is important to note that some of the princes were bearded and smaller than average!

Wanted, dead or alive

Reward: $10,000

The Wolf

Misdeeds
- Extremely dangerous individual with a legendary appetite
- Attacks and devours sheep, little pigs, grandmothers, and sometimes mischievous children

Description
His distinctive features include large eyes, large ears, and large teeth.

Anecdote

In the sleepy village of Mirepeix Bois Joli, a frightening notice appeared overnight, posted on every oak tree and lamp post. "Wanted dead or alive. Reward: 10,000 louis d'or. The Wolf," it declared in bold letters, causing quite a stir among the villagers who read it with palpable concern.

The wolf in question was no ordinary beast. With eyes as wide as saucers, ears that could hear a pin drop in the next village, and teeth that could—and did—gnaw through even the sturdiest of femurs, he was a legend. A gourmet at heart, he preferred the finer things in life: large, fluffy sheep with a taste of mint; the occasional fat and sweet-smelling grandmother; and, for dessert, the rare mischievous child who thought it wise to wander into the woods past their bedtime.

But what the poster failed to mention was the wolf's other, less fearsome side. You see, this wolf had a peculiar penchant for pastry, a soft spot for strudel, and a love for langue de chat biscuits. He often left the scene of the "crime" with a dusting of flour on his snout and icing on his paws.

The reward went unclaimed; for every time a brave soul ventured into the woods to catch the wolf, they found themselves instead sharing a margarita and tales of gastronomic adventures with the most charming, if slightly roguish, creature they had ever met.

The villagers never did get their reward, but they gained a new friend. And the sheep? Well, they learned to sleep with one eye open, as a few of them kept disappearing, the wolf's appetite returning to nature from time to time.

Wanted, dead or alive

Reward: 1,000 deniers

The Fox

Misdeeds
- Individual without faith or law
- Sly, a trickster, and a swindler
- Often found singing old Brittany folk songs at night with the wolf and the weasel

Anecdote

In the quiet hamlet of Trans La Forêt in Brittany, there lived a fox so cunning he became the stuff of legend. This fox, named Bocage, was not your ordinary four-legged prowler. No, he was a master of mischief and a virtuoso of vexation. The villagers had long since given up on simple traps and hunts; Bocage was too clever by half and had outwitted them all.

His exploits were many. He'd slip into the henhouses not just to pilfer a plump hen or two but to leave behind a feathered carpet, crafted from their own feathers, as if to add insult to injury.

The mayor, a wise man known by his first name, Mika, commissioned a poster offering a reward of 1,000 deniers for the capture of the fox, dead or alive. Bocage, with a twinkle in his eye, saw the poster as the ultimate challenge. He took on the challenge and secretly orchestrated a feast, inviting his best friends, the wolf and the weasel, to dine on the finest stolen cheeses and fruits, all under the noses of the slumbering townsfolk.

Bocage's pièce de résistance came on a moonlit night when he swiped a banjo from a traveling band. Perched atop the town's oldest oak, he strummed and sang tales of his own grandeur until the sun's first light. With a voice as smooth as aged wine, he crooned love ballads so touching that even the most chaste of maidens found themselves blushing. The villagers, half in awe and half in irritation, could only shake their fists as they were serenaded.

To this day, the legend of Bocage grows, each retelling more embellished than the last. And that Wanted poster? It's become the most treasured artwork in the local tavern, a reminder of the fox who outfoxed them all. Even nowadays, it is said that by moonlight in the forest, some people have been very lucky to see the fox, the wolf, and the weasel singing and dancing under the tall oak trees.

Wanted, dead or alive

Reward: 100 mice

Sexy Cat

Description
This wanted cat is a little less sexually unattractive than our friend Garfield.

I am less spiritual than that big, clumsy, fat cat Garfield, but I have more success with the cool Molly cats.

Anecdote

In the quaint village of Dar GaChât, there was quite the stir when the local bulletin board featured an unusual poster. It was a Wanted ad, unlike any other, seeking a feline of particular charm: Chat Sexy. This cat was no ordinary cat; it had the swagger of a movie star, with a cheeky grin and a love for tailored pants.

The reward for this cat's capture? A hundred mice—a fortune in the rodent economy. The villagers whispered rumors as they passed by the poster.

"They say he's less spiritual than a cheeseburger," Madam Braguette would whisper, adjusting her spectacles.

"But he has more success with the ladies than the town's mayor," added Mademoiselle Zobinette, who had caressed more than a few cats, as one could hear on market days.

Yet what really caught the eye was the artist's signature—a spider named René Mugnier, adding a touch of sophistication to the comical affair with its delicate web in the corner. The story of Chat Sexy became the talk of the town. Everyone wondered who might be the brave soul to bring in this charismatic cat, hopefully alive. Would it be for the mice, the glory, or just to see if Chat Sexy was as suave as the poster promised?

As autumn leaves began to fall, Chat Sexy remained at large, his legend growing with each passing day. Some say he was a myth, a legend spun by René the spider, while others swore they'd seen a dapper cat with pocket-watch pants winking at them from the back alley or on a roof of the village.

The tale of Chat Sexy lived on, a funny story beneath a drawing that brought laughter and a touch of mystery to the village of Dar GaChât.

Wanted, dead or alive

Reward: 1,000 marks

Robin Hood

Misdeeds
- an arrogant thief
- the chief of a gang of rascals

Description
    He wears green tights and hides in the forest.

Yes, indeed, it was nice to rob the rich to give a little to the poor. During these difficult periods, we are forced to rob even the poor just to survive. I hope we won't be forced to work.

Anecdote

Deep in the forest of Sherwood, where the trees whispered ancient secrets and the wind sang of yore, there stood an unusual gathering. A band of very old merry men led by a still cocky but somewhat matured Robin of the Woods. Now, this wasn't your typical Robin Hood; this was Robin with a bushy white beard and a dwindling reputation as patched as his outfit, with still a passion for green tights—so much so that he refused to acknowledge any fashion trends post-twelfth century.

A poster for his capture, dead or alive, had gone viral for years, if one could say so for medieval standards. It had been nailed to every tree and tavern door, offering a hefty sum of one thousand marks for Robin's capture, dead or alive. By now the money had lost much of its attraction because of the devaluation, and you'd be lucky to buy a goat with that sum now.

But catching him was not an easy task. The forest was no ordinary thicket; it was a labyrinth of trickery where every leaf could be an accomplice and every branch a silent guardian. On the other hand, Robin and his jolly men had aged to the point where they couldn't catch a cold, let alone the rich folks. Their horseback riding resembled a leisurely stroll more than a gallop, and they had to stop often because of their prostatic problems.

During a last supper, Robin and Maid Marian (who still had a thing for the man in green tights) gathered the gang.

Robin raised a toast. "To the rich and the poor we've 'borrowed' from." He chuckled with a wink. "May they find enough humor to forget our names and our IOUs!"

As dawn crept in, the gang left with full bellies and the beginning of a hangover, jokingly hoping they had saved enough money during their younger years and wouldn't have to get day jobs. After all, in Sherwood, work was a four-letter word, and the later years of the gang will never be recorded nor become part of the legend of Robin of the Woods, whose exaggerated flamboyant reputation from his younger life will live forever.

Wanted, dead or alive

Reward: $100

The "Basement Rat"

Misdeeds
  He uses nontraditional methods to give life to constructions deemed destroyed.

Anecdote

In the picturesque town of Beantown, a legend circulated among the crumbling old buildings. They spoke of the mysterious Basement Rat. This wasn't your garden-variety rodent but an old structural engineer so unorthodox in his professional execution that he had become an urban myth.

Authorities had posted wanted posters: "Wanted, dead or alive. Reward: $100." The crime? Brazenly rescuing the buildings that so-called sane folks and greedy developers had sentenced to demolition. The outlaw in question was a well-known octogenarian recognized for his black uniform and a pencil always hanging over his shirt collar.

His methods were unconventional, mixing ancient knowledge with an infallible intuition for structural integrity. He could listen to the aching bones of a building and diagnose its troubles. He wielded a measuring tape with the finesse of a maestro conducting an orchestra, diagnosing structural ailments with dramatic flair and occasionally lecturing a contractor with a South Mediterranean accent for good measure.

With more years under his belt than an old Bordeaux wine, he had a knack for whispering sweet nothings to the creakiest structures and the most fatigued of foundations. He'd take a shack on the brink of collapse, one stiff breeze away from becoming matchsticks, and *poof!* It'd be reborn as a chic *chez moi*, ready for a glossy magazine's front page.

The secret of the Basement Rat? He knew every basement in Boston, and rumor had it that every brick and beam had a story he could unravel. The Rat cherry-picked his adventures, taking on the jobs that made other engineers sweat just from a glance at the blueprints.

His reputation grew. Stories of his feats were told in hushed tones in the dusty corners of Brattle Street pubs. They said he once realigned the beams of a leaning house back to dignity with nothing more than a handful of nails and an iron will. Another time, he reportedly straightened a sagging roof crushed by snow, lifting it with his own hands. City officials were torn between giving him a medal or a mugshot, while the townsfolk regarded him as the Robin Hood of renovations. They knew that if the Rat took on their case, their beloved home would not only be repaired; it would be revitalized, filled with stories and laughter.

Thus, the legend of the Basement Rat endured, with every building he touched standing a little prouder, each beam buzzing with the secret of having regained its lost capacity.

And the Rat? Well, he would wink, adjust his glasses, pick up his bread, and disappear into the labyrinth of the city he loved, always one step ahead, always in search of the next mission impossible.

It's rumored that in the deepest, darkest basements, archaeologists have discovered the ancient bones of corrupt civil servants. Legend has it, these were the ones bold enough to try to blackmail him. These number-crunching warriors had been known to threaten his integrity. So remember, if you're thinking of crossing him, you better be good at playing hide-and-seek—permanently!

Here is a list of several graphic novel and illustrated book publishers, including their locations. For specific addresses and phone numbers, you'll need to visit their websites or contact them directly:

1. **Archie Comics**: A leading publisher in the comic book industry, known for iconic characters like Archie and Sabrina the Teenage Witch. Location: New York City, US. [Submission Guidelines] (archiecomics.com) [oai_citation:1,Error] (data:text/plain;charset=utf-8,Unable%20to%20find%20metadata).

2. **Kodansha Comics**: A major publisher of English-language manga as well as other fiction and non-fiction from Japan. Location: New York City, US. [Website] (https://kodansha.us) [oai_citation:2,Error](data:text/plain;charset=utf-8,Unable%20to%20find%20metadata).

3. **First Second Books**: A New York City-based graphic novel publisher specializing in a wide range of genres. [Submission Guidelines] (firstsecondbooks.com) [oai_citation:3,Error](data:text/plain;charset=utf-8,Unable%20to%20find%20metadata).

4. **Titan Comics**: Part of Titan Publishing, specializing in new comic stories and handling licensed film and television properties. [Submission Guidelines] (titancomics-wanted.tumblr.com) [oai_citation:4,Error] (data:text/ plain;charset=utf-8,Unable%20to%20find%20metadata).

5. **Yen Press**: An English-language comics publisher, part of a joint venture between Hachette Group and Kodansha Comics. [Submission Guidelines] (yenpress.com) [oai_citation:5,Error](data:text/ plain;charset=utf-8,Unable%20to%20find%20metadata).

6. **Oni Press**: A publisher based in Portland, Oregon, known for a diverse portfolio of comic books and graphic novels. [Submission Guidelines] (onipress.submittable.com) [oai_citation:6,Error](data:text/ plain;charset=utf-8,Unable%20to%20find%20metadata).

7. **Drawn & Quarterly**: A Canadian publisher specializing in comics and graphic novels. [Submission Guidelines](drawnandquarterly.com)[oai_citation:7,Error](data:text/plain;charset=utf8,Unable%20to%20find%20metadata).

8. **Fantagraphics**: An established graphic novel publisher with a focus on both classic and contemporary artists. [Website](www.fantagraphics.com) [oai_citation:8,Error](data:text/plain;charset=utf-8,Unable%20to%20find%20metadata).

9. **IDW Publishing**: Known for popular titles and reaching new audiences. [Website](www.idwpublishing.com)[oai_citation:9,Error](data:text/plain;charset=utf8,Unable%20to%20find%20metadata).

10. **Top Shelf**: An imprint of IDW, focusing on sophisticated and visionary graphic novels. [Website](www.topshelfcomix.com)[oai_citation:10,Error](data:text/plain;charset=utf8,Unable%20to%20find%20metadata).

11. **Vertigo Comics**: An imprint of DC, specializing in adult fantasy comics. [Website](www.dc.com) [oai_citation:11,Error](data:text/plain;charset=utf-8,Unable%20to%20find%20metadata).

12. **Quirk Books**: An independent publisher with a curated list of unconventional titles. Location: Philadelphia, US. [Submission Format] (www.quirkbooks.com) [oai_citation:12,47 Top Comics & Graphic Novels Book Publishers in 2024 | Reedsy](https://blog.reedsy.com/publishers/comics-graphic-novels/) [oai_citation:13,Error](data:text/ plain;charset=utf-8,Unable%20to%20find%20metadata).

13. **Talos Press**: An imprint of Skyhorse Publishing, focusing on fantasy, horror, and sci-fi. Location: New York City, US. [Submission Format] (www.skyhorsepublishing.com) [oai_citation:14,47 Top Comics & Graphic Novels Book Publishers in 2024 | Reedsy](https://blog.reedsy.com/publishers/comics-graphic-novels/) [oai_citation:15,Error](data:text/plain;charset=utf-8,Unable%20to%20find%20metadata).

These publishers vary in size and genre specialization, so researching their submission guidelines and catalogues to find the best fit for your work is recommended.

About the Author

With a legacy spanning over fifty years, Rene Mugnier blends engineering experience with whimsical artistry in his drawings, each accompanied by witty commentaries. His books and drawings offer a glimpse at a lifetime of humorous observations and artistic creations. Through these pages, discover the essence of a life lived with humor and insight.

Printed in the USA
CPSIA information can be obtained
at www.ICGtesting.com
CBRC090908061024
15321CB00090B/1207